BUILDING BLOCKS OF MATH

SUBTRACTION

Written by Joseph Midthun

Illustrated by Samuel Hiti

WORLD BOOK

a Scott Fetzer company
Chicago

World Book, Inc.
180 North LaSalle Street
Suite 900
Chicago, Illinois 60601
USA

For information about other World Book publications,
visit our website at **www.worldbook.com**
or call **1-800-WORLDBK (967-5325).**
For information about sales to schools and libraries,
call 1-800-975-3250 (United States),
or 1-800-837-5365 (Canada).

Library of Congress Cataloging-in-Publication Data
for this volume has been applied for.

Building Blocks of Math
ISBN: 978-0-7166-4447-7 (set, hc.)

Subtraction
ISBN: 978-0-7166-4453-8 (hc.)

Also available as:
ISBN: 978-0-7166-4459-0 (e-book)

1st printing March 2022

Acknowledgments:
Created by Samuel Hiti and Joseph Midthun
Art by Samuel Hiti
Additional art by David Shephard/
    The Bright Agency
Additional spot art by Shutterstock
Text by Joseph Midthun

TABLE OF CONTENTS

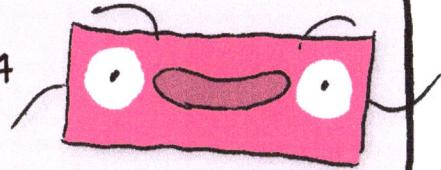

You know how to add up numbers, right?

I'm Subtraction!

Well, I look at things differently.

I help you find the difference between two amounts!

See this?

This is a subtraction problem!

If you have 3 and take away 2, what's the difference?

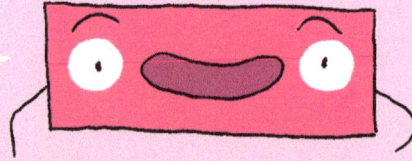

You could also write it like this:

Squeak

Say you have 3 triangles and take away 2...

The difference is 1 triangle!

Squeak

Squeak

You can use me in all kinds of ways!

Come on. I'll show you!

13, 14, 15, 16.

Hey Addition!

What are you doing?

Counting peaches!

I have 16 peaches. Yum!

But 7 of them are rotten!

So?

So you need to get rid of them. They'll give you a stomachache.

Oh.

How many peaches will you have if we take away the 7 rotten ones?

16 − 7 = ?

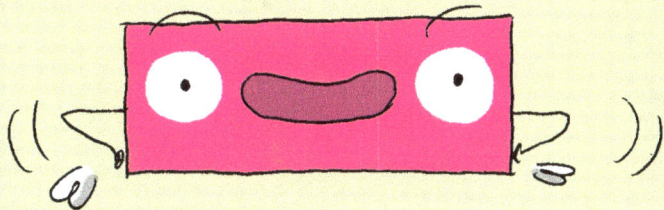

Have you ever used a number line?

A number line can help you solve equations like this one:

$$37 - 19 = ?$$

Counting back on a number line is like taking away.

Let's use the number line to help us find the answer to 37 - 19!

Where do we start?

0 1 2 3 4 5 6 7 8 9 10

Let's start on 37.

Plop

37

Now we can count back to 19 to find the answer.

Cool!

37

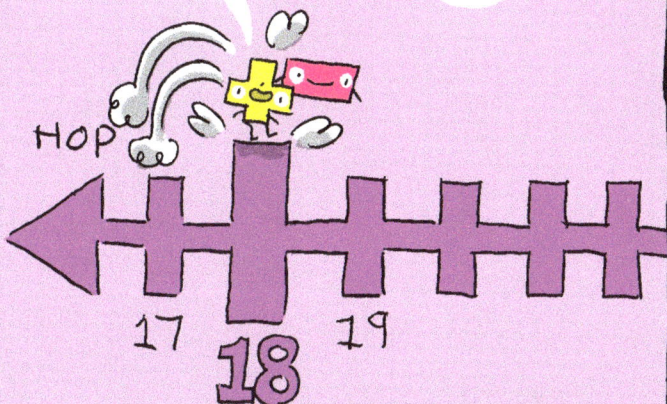

You can always use addition to check an answer you found with subtraction.

You know, we could even solve the original problem by adding.

No way!

Sure.

I'd write the problem like this:

$$19 + ? = 37$$

Now we just need to count up from 19 until we reach 37.

Lead the way.

Nice shot!

Wow, you're pretty good at playing marbles!

Practice makes perfect!

I started with 53 marbles.

Then, I lost 25 over the course of the game.

Let's count back to figure out how many I have left.

Hold on!

Could we try regrouping the numbers first?

How?

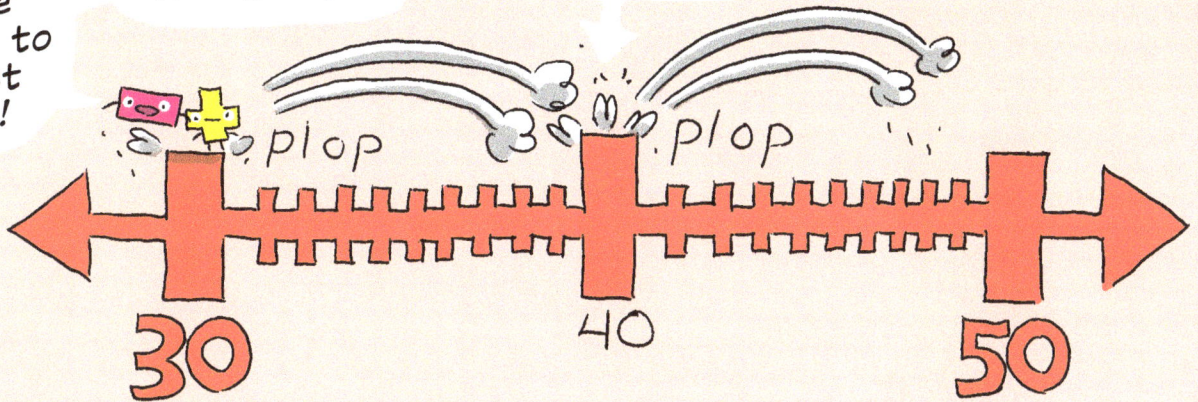

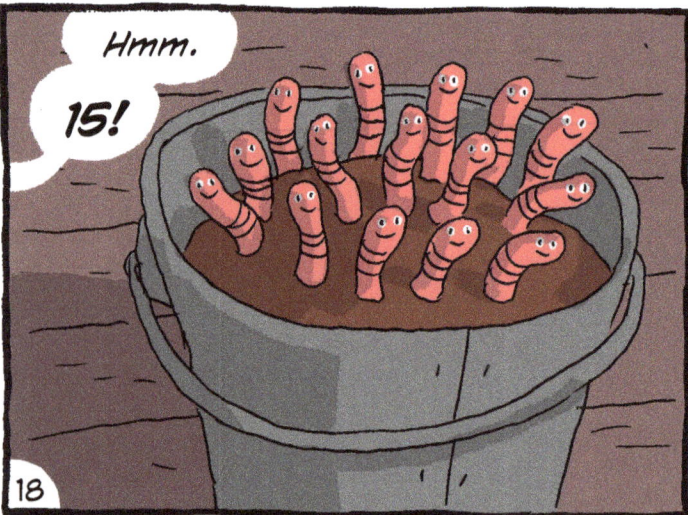

Let's look at it like this:

$$15 - ? = 8$$

FREEDOM!

We know how many worms we had at first.

And we know how many we managed to catch.

15!

8!

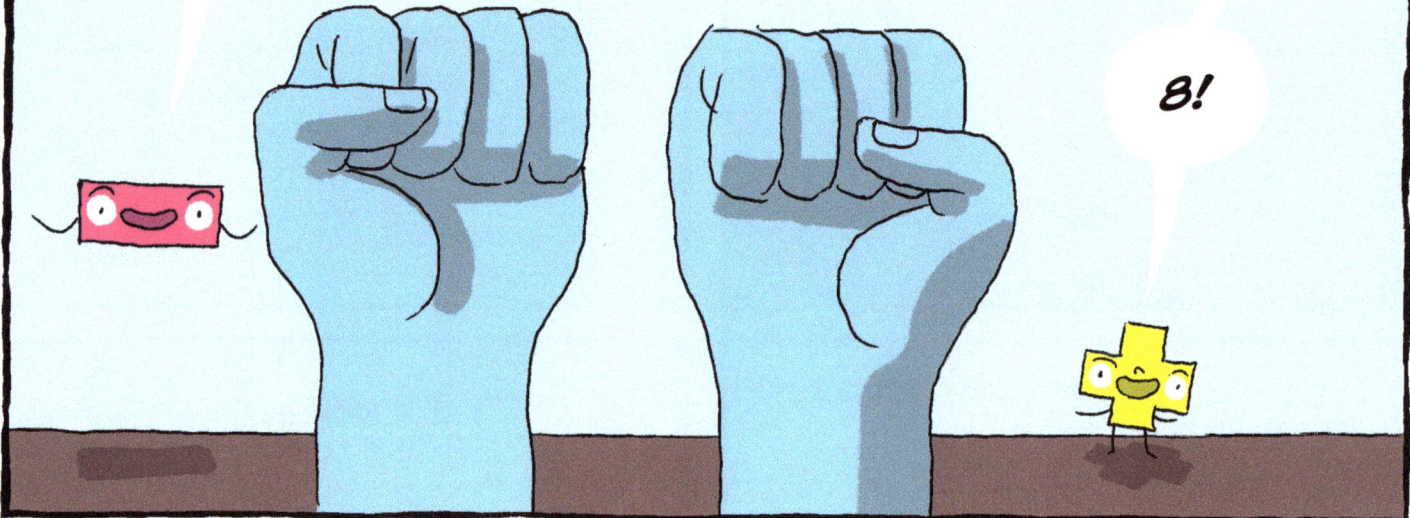

So let's start at 15 and count back to 8.
You can use your hands to keep track!

14,

13,

12,

11,

10,

9,

8.

How many
fingers are you
holding up?

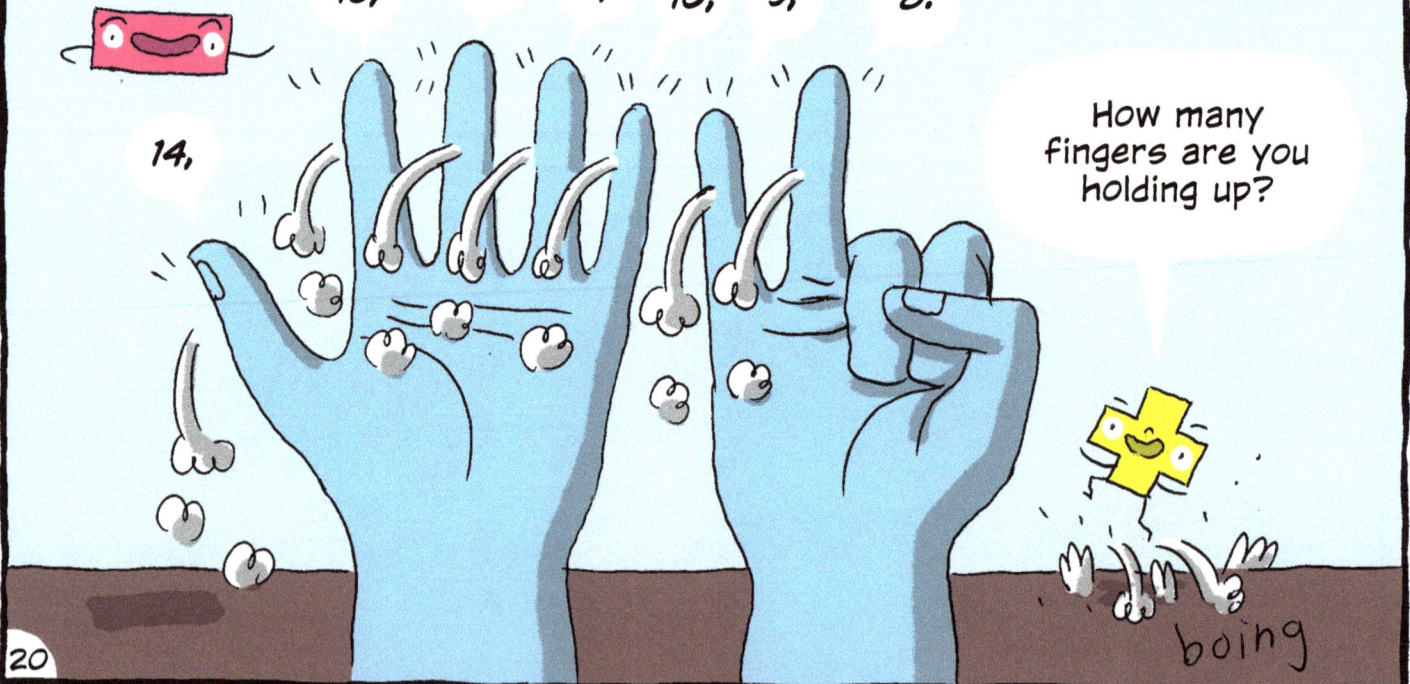

boing

21

Think of the problem like this:

$$8 + ? = 15$$

Let's use a number line to count up from 8 to 15!

plop

8   15

Most people find that 10 is easier to work with than 8.

8

So, let's add 2 to 8 to make 10.

plop, plop

8   10

What plus 10 equals 15?

5!

Let's add 5 to get 15.

ZIP

10 + 5 = 15

Now let's add the jumps to find the answer!

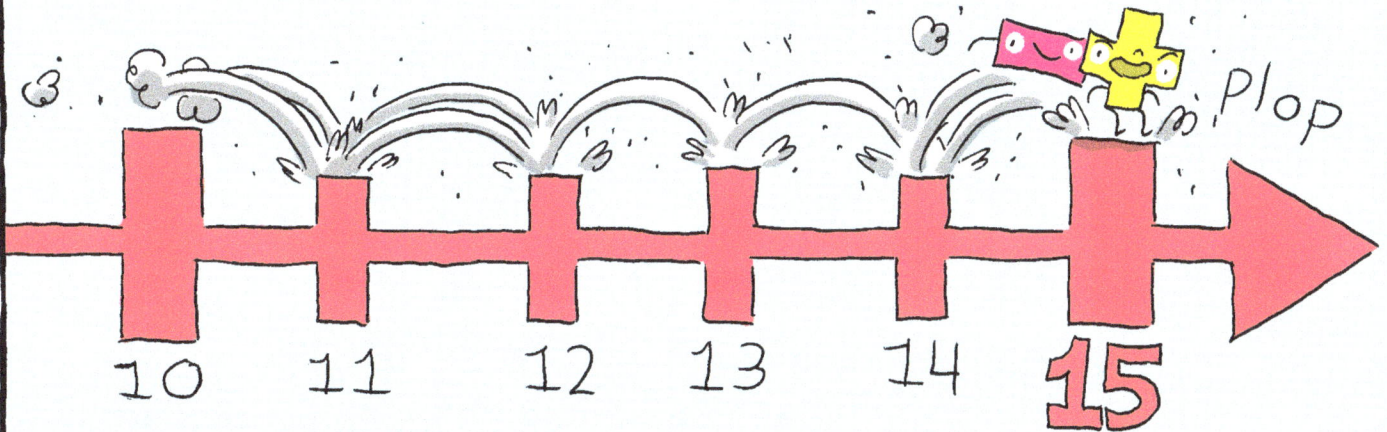

Plop

10   11   12   13   14   15

We jumped 2 and we jumped 5.

2 + 5 = 7

So, we were correct before. 15 - 7 equals 8!

You got it!

24

Let's figure it out. There were 25 cars to begin with, and we removed an unknown number...

We need to count up the remaining cars!

1, 2, 3, 4, 5, 6, 7, 8, 9, 10, 11, 12, 13, 14.

There are 14 train cars remaining!

So, we can look at the problem like this:

$$25 - ? = 14$$

If you come across a math problem you can't solve, don't give up...

Once you figure it out, you can show a friend how to do it, too!

And remember, if you ever need to find a difference, just use me!

I'm *Subtraction!*

TIMELINE

The Egyptians used a hieroglyphic number system based on the number 10.

The Babylonians developed a number system based on the number 60. We still use that system today to count minutes and seconds!

3000 B.C.

2100 B.C.

200 B.C.

A Chinese math book had the first known reference to negative numbers.

500 B.C.

2600 B.C.

The Egyptians used geometry to build the Great Pyramid of Giza.

The ancient Romans created the Roman numeral system. All Roman numerals are written using symbols, either alone or in combination, such as I for 1, V for 5, X for 10, and L for 50.

I 1 II 2 III 3

V 5 VI 6 VII 7

VIII 9 X 10

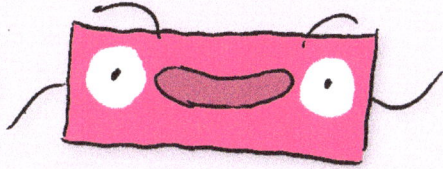

The first printed book with the plus (+) and minus (-) signs was published in Europe.

1489

French mathematician Blaise Pascal invented a calculating machine that could add and subtract.

1642

The first electronic calculators make subtraction easier.

1960's

1557

The first printed book with the equal (=) sign was published in Europe.

1790

The metric system was first developed in France.

WHO'S WHO: ADA LOVELACE

Problem 4. 79 minus 45 equals what?

Can you help me with this problem? What is 79 - 45?

34

Correct! Thanks, how did you know the correct answer?

My name is Ada Lovelace. I am a mathematician. I also wrote the first published computer program.

The first program! Did you create Pong?

No, Pong, what? Never mind, actually my program calculated a series of numbers that is important in math.

That doesn't sound as fun as Pong. Did you have computers like the ones we have today?

No, we didn't have anything like the computers you have today.

I wrote a step-by-step procedure for solving a math problem. My procedure could be used to program a machine.

Wow, you must be smart! Maybe you can help me with these problems. Let's see. Problem 5. 57 minus 26 equals what?

Fact File

Name: Ada Lovelace

Born: 1815 in London, England

Occupation: Mathematician

Claim to fame: Wrote the first published computer program.

33

ACTIVITY:
MAKE YOUR OWN ABACUS

Follow these instructions to make your own abacus!

For thousands of years people have used an abacus to count, add, and subtract.

First, you are going to need these materials.

What You'll Need
- 4 craft sticks each about 4.5 in (11.4 cm) long
- 5 bamboo skewers
- 50 pony beads
- Ruler
- Pencil
- Wood glue

Starting 1/4 in (0.6 cm) from the end of one craft stick, mark a line with your pencil every inch (2.5 cm). You should end up with 5 lines.

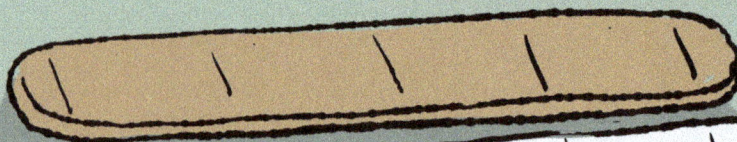

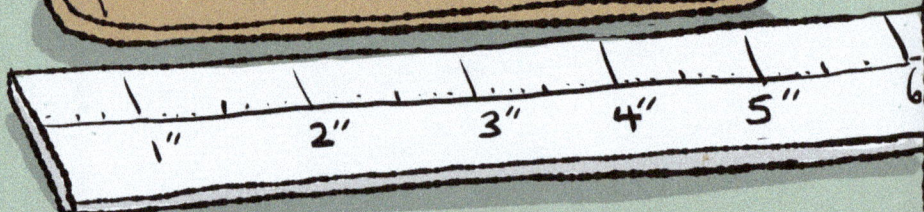

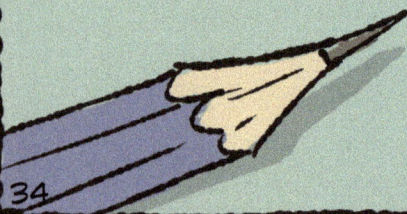

1"   2"   3"   4"   5"   6

Put glue on each of the lines. Glue the ends of each of the bamboo skewers onto the craft stick. Be sure to keep the sticks straight and parallel (same distance apart everywhere).

Next, glue a 2nd craft stick to the same end of the bamboo skewers so that they are secured between the 2 sticks. Like the image here. Let the glue dry.

Slide 10 beads onto each bamboo skewer. Like you see here.

Finally, put glue on the open ends of the bamboo skewers. Glue the last two craft sticks to the end just like the ones you've already glued at the other end. Let the glue dry.

You now have an abacus that can count big numbers. Each skewer represents a different place value: ones, tens, hundreds, thousands, and ten thousands. You can mark each column's place value at the top or bottom of you abacus.

Ten thousands

Thousands

Hundreds

Tens

Ones

Count by sliding the beads to the opposite end of the stick. Once all 10 beads have been counted, return them to the other end of the stick and slide one bead across the stick to the left to indicate an increase of 10. Try adding and subtracting using this method.

CAN YOU BELIEVE IT?!

The ancient Chinese, Greeks, and Romans

used an abacus

to solve math problems. The abacus consists of a frame containing columns of beads that represent numbers.

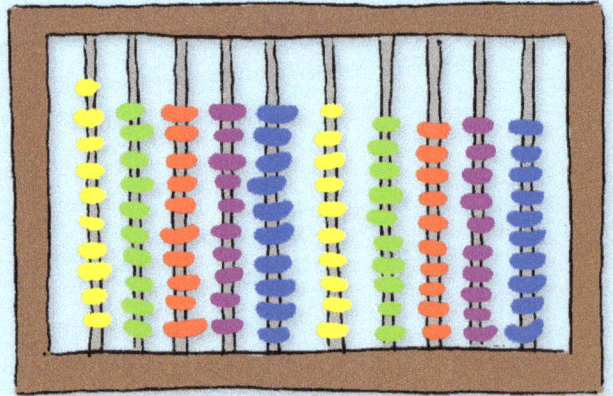

The difference

of two odd numbers is always an even number. For example, 7 - 3 = 4, 25 - 17 = 8, and 57 - 21 = 36.

In a

subtraction problem

like 8 - 3 = 5, the first number (here 8) is called the *minuend*, the second number (here 3) is called the *subtrahend*, and the answer (here 5) is called the *difference*.

In 2020, a man in India subtracted two 100-digit numbers in just under

55 seconds.

SUBTRACTION FACTS

This table below can help you add and subtract fast!
It can also help you learn your subtraction fact families.
A fact family shows how groups of numbers are related.

The table shows 10 different fact families for addition and
subtraction. Can you think of more fact families?

5 + 5 = 10 10 - 5 = 5	6 + 5 = 11 11 - 5 = 6 11 - 6 = 5	7 + 5 = 12 12 - 5 = 7 12 - 7 = 5	8 + 5 = 13 13 - 5 = 8 13 - 8 = 5	9 + 5 = 14 14 - 5 = 9 14 - 9 = 5
5 + 6 = 11 11 - 6 = 5 11 - 5 = 6	6 + 6 = 12 12 - 6 = 6	7 + 6 = 13 13 - 6 = 7 13 - 7 = 6	8 + 6 = 14 14 - 6 = 8 14 - 8 = 6	9 + 6 = 15 15 - 6 = 9 15 - 9 = 6
5 + 7 = 12 12 - 7 = 5 12 - 5 = 7	6 + 7 = 13 13 - 7 = 6 13 - 6 = 7	7 + 7 = 14 14 - 7 = 7	8 + 7 = 15 15 - 7 = 8 15 - 8 = 7	9 + 7 = 16 16 - 7 = 9 16 - 9 = 7
5 + 8 = 13 13 - 8 = 5 13 - 5 = 8	6 + 8 = 14 14 - 8 = 6 14 - 6 = 8	7 + 8 = 15 15 - 8 = 7 15 - 7 = 8	8 + 8 = 16 16 - 8 = 8	9 + 8 = 17 17 - 8 = 9 17 - 9 = 8
5 + 9 = 14 14 - 9 = 5 14 - 5 = 9	6 + 9 = 15 15 - 9 = 6 15 - 6 = 9	7 + 9 = 16 16 - 9 = 7 16 - 7 = 9	8 + 9 = 17 17 - 9 = 8 17 - 8 = 9	9 + 9 = 18 18 - 9 = 9

NOTE TO EDUCATORS

This volume supports a conceptual understanding of subtraction through a series of story problems. As the Subtraction character solves each story problem, it presents different strategies, including variations of direct modeling, counting, and invented strategies. Below is an index of strategies that appear in this volume.

Index of Strategies

Index

www.ingramcontent.com/pod-product-compliance
Lightning Source LLC
Chambersburg PA
CBHW061411090426
42741CB00021B/3486